SHENANDOAH VALLEY

impressions

Photography and text by Pat and Chuck Blackley

Pat & Chuck Blackley
2004

FARCOUNTRY
PRESS

Right: At Goshen Pass in Rockbridge County, the Maury River flows through a scenic three-mile canyon in the Allegheny Mountains.

Title page: The Dry Run United Church of Christ at Fort Valley in Shenandoah County is typical of the small country churches along the Valley's back roads.

Front cover: Autumn leaves bathed in early morning sunlight frame a farm near Moscow in Augusta County.

Back cover: As the Shenandoah River winds lazily along its course in Page County, another day in the Valley draws to a close.

ISBN 1-56037-287-7
Photographs © by Pat and Chuck Blackley
© 2004 Farcountry Press

Created, produced, and designed in the United States.
Printed in China.

INTRODUCTION

by Pat and Chuck Blackley

Cradled between the Blue Ridge Mountains to the east and the Allegheny Mountains to the west lies the Shenandoah Valley of the Virginias. This is a land blessed with fertile, rolling farmland, acres of lush woodlands, and clear, rushing streams and rivers.

According to one early-American legend, thought to be based on a Native American legend, the stars in the heavens were so awed by the beauty of the valley below them that they plucked the brightest jewels from their crowns and tossed them down into the river, where they continued to sparkle and shine, thus giving the river and its valley their name: Shenandoah—Clear-Eyed Daughter of the Stars.

The Valley, strictly defined, is the area within the watershed of the Shenandoah River, a region that stretches approximately 150 miles from the river's southernmost source in northern Rockbridge County to its northern terminus at Harpers Ferry, where it empties into the Potomac.

But, in practice, the Valley's boundaries extend well beyond that limited geographic area. Today's Valley is defined more by economics, culture, and lifestyle. The boundaries are widened to include a total of sixteen counties in an area that runs from the Potomac River in West Virginia southward to Roanoke, Virginia (the Valley's largest city), and from the Blue Ridge Mountains west across the Alleghenies to the West Virginia border.

The Shenandoah Valley and the mountains that flank it were formed hundreds of millions of years ago by a succession of geological events. In fact, the Appalachians, of which the Blue Ridge and Allegheny chains are a part, rank among the oldest mountains in the world, at between 250 and 300 million years old. Though, at one time, these mountains were probably as high as the Alps, millennia of weathering have worn them down to their more modest size today.

With the exception of trappers and transient bands of Native Americans, this western frontier of Virginia, which was isolated from the rest of the colony by its formidable mountains, remained unsettled until the eighteenth century. In the late 1600s and early 1700s, Germans, including Quakers and Mennonites, left their homeland because of religious persecution and settled in Pennsylvania. These came to be known as the "Pennsylvania Dutch," *Dutch* being a corruption of *Deutsche,* meaning German. Meanwhile, immigrants in Ireland, who had fled persecution in their homeland of Scotland, were again mistreated in their new country and were forced to move once more, this time across the ocean to Pennsylvania. They were known as the Scotch-Irish. Both groups, in their continuing search for land suitable for farming and assurances of economic, religious, and political equality, made their way down from Pennsylvania, entering the Valley after crossing the Potomac at what is now Shepardstown, West Virginia. These were strong, religious, industrious people who came to the Valley with little but their dreams and determination to make a new and better life for themselves and their families.

The last to settle in the Valley during those early years were the English. These were mostly prominent families in Tidewater who came west across the mountains, in smaller numbers, looking to increase their land holdings or begin large farming operations.

What those early Valley settlers found when they arrived was a land rich in natural resources and wildlife. The fertile soils responded to their hard work, and the fields burst into life, yielding abundant crops of wheat, corn, beans, and potatoes. Farms were soon spreading across the landscape. Cattle and sheep fattened in lush green pastures. Hillside orchards produced bushels of luscious apples, peaches, plums, and cherries. The land became an agricultural promised land, and the people prospered.

Those early settlers brought with them the lifestyles and habits of their mother countries. They each had their own religious practices, their own music, their own recipes. But over the years, they blended together into a more homogenous culture—one that, while unified, still held onto its family roots. They worked together to build their communities, while striving to preserve those unique traits and practices that made them individuals. Thus was born "the Valley way of life."

It wasn't always easy. Years of peaceful existence were interrupted by years of war and strife. Valley citizens rallied during the French and Indian, Revolutionary, and Civil wars, many making the ultimate sacrifice. During the Civil War especially, the Valley suffered a terrible price, both in lives and property lost. The Valley's fruitful soils had earned it the reputation as "the Breadbasket of the Confederacy" since they supplied the Southern army with much of its food supplies. As a result, in 1864, the Union undertook "the burning," a campaign that destroyed the Valley's barns, mills, crops, and livestock.

Facing page: Blooming fencerow with farm, Swoope, Augusta County.

But the years of war could not break the spirit of those tenacious Valley residents, and the post-war era found them rebounding and rebuilding that which they had lost.

The Shenandoah Valley today, although it has grown and opened its doors to many other cultures, still holds onto its "Valley way of life." And while it has marched admirably into the future, it still holds a strong affinity for the past. This can be observed throughout the Valley in its preserved and lovingly restored architecture; the museums that explain its origins and honor its heroes; the battlefields and reenactments that strive to portray accurately a painful and sometimes misunderstood time in history; and the ethnic festivals that celebrate the traditional aspects of Valley life through food, music, and crafts. It can also be seen in the family farms that keep agriculture a major part of the Valley economy and the quaint towns and villages that welcome visitors with cozy bed-and-breakfasts, down-home cooking, and antique stores bursting with treasures from the past.

The Valley has also worked hard to preserve the wealth of its natural resources within the protected boundaries of Shenandoah National Park, the Blue Ridge Parkway, and the Washington and Jefferson National Forests, thus providing abundant opportunities for fishing, boating, camping, and hiking. More recently, preserving the Valley's character has taken on increasing importance.

Today's Shenandoah is not just a place. It's much more than green, fertile farmlands stretched out between gentle, blue mountains. It's more than the rivers and caverns and hot springs. It's a complete story, filled with people, history, challenges, sufferings, and prosperities. And it all unites to form a very special place, indeed. Shenandoah—Clear-Eyed Daughter of the Stars.

★   ★   ★   ★   ★

Picture this: You are standing on the Blue Ridge Parkway, looking west. Spread before you is a patchwork quilt of farmland and small towns stitched together by the Shenandoah and James rivers and their tributaries. Your eyes take in a landscape representing generations of family farms and forests, the bones of the history of our nation, and unspoiled natural resources special to the Shenandoah Valley region.

Shenandoah Valley Impressions, by lifelong Valley residents Pat and Chuck Blackley, is a vivid depiction of the essence of Virginia's Shenandoah Valley—the very land we are committed to preserving. The Blackleys' commitment to the Valley brings this beautiful book to you. This same commitment also brings information about Valley Conservation Council to *Shenandoah Valley Impressions* readers. We are grateful for the images of the Valley preserved through their work and for the Blackleys' generous invitation to tell you about VCC and our efforts to preserve the Valley through land protection.

As the Shenandoah Valley's only regional land trust, Valley Conservation Council is committed to protecting our rural heritage. We work with landowners, local officials, and private citizens to advance a new way of thinking—one that joins far-sighted and creative development to preserve our native fields and forests. Our land ethic envisions strong local economies flourishing amid working farms and wildlife habitat, rather than displacing them.

For information:

Valley Conservation Council
17-19 Barristers Row
Staunton, VA 24401
(540) 886-3541
www.valleyconservation.org

Facing page: In the early eighteenth century, Quaker Abram Hollingsworth purchased 582 acres from a group of Shawnees he found camped by a natural spring in what is now Winchester. He built a log cabin and gristmill on the site, and later his son Isaac built a larger limestone house. Both the restored cabin and the 1754 house (oldest in Winchester) can be visited at the Abrams Delight Museum.

Above: Known affectionately by locals as the Mole Hill, the vantage point for this view near Dayton is actually an extinct volcano. Mennonite farms dot the landscape here, which many believe to be the most picturesque spot in Rockingham County.

Right: Rockingham County Courthouse graces Court Square in downtown Harrisonburg.

Facing Page: Twilight turns the sky pink as a full moon rises above an Augusta County farm.

Above: Virginia Military Institute cadets raise the VMI flag during an annual reenactment of the Battle of New Market. In May 1864, young cadets from VMI left their studies and marched from Lexington to New Market to reinforce the dwindling Southern ranks. There, on May 15, they bravely took to the battlefield in what was one of the last Confederate victories in the Valley.

Left: The son of a Presbyterian minister, Woodrow Wilson was born in 1856 in this manse in Staunton. He would later become our twenty-eighth president.

Above: Morning sunlight pierces the autumn foliage surrounding McKinley Methodist Church in Augusta County.

Right: Dubbed "the Switzerland of Virginia," Highland County lies nestled within the western ridges of the Allegheny Mountains. Geographically remote and sparsely populated, it is often said that the county's sheep population exceeds its human one.

13

Above: A statue of Confederate general Thomas "Stonewall" Jackson marks his grave in Lexington. Before he was called for duty in the Civil War, Jackson was a professor of physics and artillery tactics at Virginia Military Institute.

Left: Canoeists enjoy a leisurely paddle down the river at Shenandoah River State Park in Warren County.

Above: The revitalized downtown of Staunton, the "Queen City," is a showcase of beautifully restored Victorian architecture. It was one of five recipients of the Great American Main Street Award, presented by the National Trust for Historic Preservation.

Right: The headwaters of the Potomac and James rivers meet here at Hightown in Highland County. It is said that on a certain barn in town, rain draining from the roof's north side runs to the Potomac and from its south side runs to the James.

Above: In Page County, the Cliffs at Compton help to form one of the most scenic stretches of the South Fork of the Shenandoah River.

Left: Belle Boyd, an authoress and actress, is best remembered for her real-life role as a Confederate spy during the Civil War. Her house (built by her father in 1853) in Martinsburg, West Virginia, is now the home of the Berkeley County Historical Society.

Facing page: Sunlight obscured by morning fog casts a warm glow on a dairy farm near Dayton in Rockingham County.

Above: Named for its mineral springs or "baths," Bath County, along with Highland and Alleghany counties, lies in the mountainous western region of the Valley known as the Alleghany Highlands. The tiny town of Warm Springs, Bath's county seat, is surrounded by pristine countryside.

Left: At Natural Chimneys Regional Park near Mount Solon in Augusta County, seven limestone pinnacles or "chimneys" rise to 120 feet above the Valley floor. They are all that remains of an ancient collapsed cavern.

Above: As a young man, George Washington used this cabin in Winchester as an office while he was surveying and guarding Virginia's western frontier. First settled in 1732, Winchester is the oldest city west of the Blue Ridge.

Right: An apple-red barn brightens up a farm on Apple Pie Ridge Road in Frederick County.

Above: Working seventeenth- and eighteenth-century farm-steads from Ireland, England, and Germany, along with a nine-teenth-century American homestead, were dismantled and transported to Staunton, where they were reassembled at the Frontier Culture Museum. Here, visitors learn about the origins and lifestyles of the Valley's early settlers.

Left: Historic Harpers Ferry, West Virginia, seen here from atop Maryland Heights, sits at the confluence of the Potomac and Shenandoah rivers and marks the northern gateway to the Shenandoah Valley.

Above: Falling Springs Falls pours over a mountainside cliff in Alleghany County. Half of this county, situated in the Allegheny Mountains, is within the George Washington National Forest.

Right: Hay bales await pick-up in this serene pastoral scene at Mossy Creek in Augusta County. Here, the rolling farmland appears to stretch without interruption all the way to the Allegheny Mountains.

Above: Midway rides light up the evening at the Rockingham County Agricultural Fair, rated as one of the ten best rural county fairs in the country.

Left: A farm near New Hope in Augusta County. On cool mornings, fog often covers the Valley like a shroud.

Above: Sugar tap and bucket, Eagle's Sugar Camp, Highland County. As the county with the highest mean elevation east of the Mississippi, Highland contains large stands of sugar maples. In early spring, the sap is collected for syrup production.

Right: Built in 1835 as part of the Kanawha Turnpike, the Humpback Bridge near Covington in Alleghany County is Virginia's oldest covered bridge, as well as the only curve-span covered bridge still remaining in the United States.

Above: When General Robert E. Lee's faithful horse Traveller died, Lee had him buried outside of his office at the Lee Chapel on the campus of Washington College (now Washington and Lee University) in Lexington, where he served as president after the Civil War. It's a long-standing tradition for visitors to leave apples and coins on Traveller's grave.

Facing page: Established in 1839, Virginia Military Institute in Lexington became the country's first state-supported military college. Over the years, VMI has produced an impressive roster of military leaders, including General George C. Marshall.

Above: The Virginia Museum of Transportation in downtown Roanoke occupies a restored railway freight station at the Norfolk Southern mainline. Indoor and outdoor exhibits tell the story of transportation in the Valley, ranging from carriages, trucks, and automobiles to trains and airplanes.

Left: Founded in 1749 and saved from bankruptcy in 1796 by a gift of stock from George Washington, Washington and Lee University is the sixth-oldest university in the nation. The front campus colonnade, with its stately columns and pilasters, is a National Historic Landmark.

Above: At the Andre Viette Farm and Nursery near Fishersville in Augusta County, thousands of flower-loving visitors arrive annually to admire an impressive array of perennials, including poppies, irises, peonies, and more than 1,000 varieties of daylilies.

Right: Open pastures in Bath County provide a peaceful setting for the Woodland Union Church.

Above: Civil War battle reenactments take place throughout the Valley. One of the most celebrated is held each May at the New Market Battlefield. Here, a family in period costume takes part in the activities.

Left: On the South Fork of the Shenandoah River in Page County, kayakers pause before entering the Compton Rapid. Paddlers are cautioned to wear their life vests in this "strong Class II rapid, which terminates in very deep water next to the cliff."

Above: Built in 1855, the Berkeley County Courthouse, with its impressive dome and pressed-tin ceilings, adorns downtown Martinsburg, West Virginia.

Right: Spring bloom at the J. P. Russell Apple Orchard in Frederick County near Winchester is an impressive sight. Frederick County is the leading apple-producing county in Virginia, harvesting more than three million bushels per year. For nearly 80 years, Winchester has hosted the famous Apple Blossom Festival, one of the largest events in the state.

Above: "8 Maples Barn" near Fincastle in Botetourt County. A quiet, mostly rural county today, Botetourt (pronounced "bot-a-tot") was once a bustling trade depot, owing to its strategic location along the James River.

Facing page: The State Arboretum of Virginia in Clarke County near Millwood is filled with gardens of boxwoods, herbs, and perennial flowers. Beautiful Clarke County remains largely rural, with dairy and beef cattle operations as well as magnificent horse farms.

Above: The low evening sun casts a soft glow on the historic railroad station at Luray in Page County. Due to its relatively remote location, tucked away between the Blue Ridge and Massanutten mountains, Page County remains largely rural. The population of its county seat, Luray, is only 4,500 people.

Right: As the sun rises over an Augusta County dairy farm, silage wagons wait silently for the day's work to begin.

Above: At Shenandoah River State Park in Warren County, blue bells herald the arrival of spring.

Left: Old Order Mennonites make their way home after Sunday service at their nearby meeting house. The Valley has a thriving Mennonite population, concentrated west of the town of Dayton in southwestern Rockingham County.

Above: Awaiting harvest, these grapes are at Rockbridge Vineyard near Raphine in Rockbridge County, one of six wineries in the Valley. Wine production has become a major industry in Virginia, with more than eighty licensed wineries, producing an impressive selection of award-winning wines.

Right: View from inside Meems Bottom Bridge in Shenandoah County. The single-span Burr-arch-truss covered bridge, originally constructed in 1892 to span the North Fork of the Shenandoah River, is the longest in the state.

Above: The historic Roanoke farmers market was established in downtown Roanoke in 1882. Nowadays, the market building is filled with eclectic restaurants and shops, and during growing season vendors fill the outdoor stalls with a colorful profusion of fresh fruits, vegetables, and plants.

Facing page: Skyline Drive in Shenandoah National Park winds 105 miles along the crest of the Blue Ridge Mountains, rewarding travelers with stunning views of the Valley below, like this one at Browntown Overlook.

Above: Orchards abound in Berkeley County, West Virginia, producing luscious bounties of apples, peaches, plums, and cherries. Many provide baskets and ladders so you can "pick your own."

Left: At Hightown, in Highland County, sheep roam the rolling pastures, grazing on the lush green grass of spring.

Above: An old steel truss bridge crosses North River near Stokesville in Augusta County. These relics are rapidly being replaced.

Right: Country lanes wind their way through peaceful farmlands in Highland County. In autumn, Highland's sugar maples provide spectacular leaf viewing, rivaling that found in New England.

Above: General store at Mauzy in Rockingham County. Even with the influx of large grocery and retail stores, small general stores still provide needed supplies in the rural areas of the Valley.

Left: As late summer brings a hint of yellow to the fields, a barefoot Mennonite girl checks the mail at a farm near Dayton in Rockingham County.

Above: Fireman statue at the Virginia Museum of Transportation in Roanoke.

Right: A summer rain swells the Falls on Jennings Creek, near Arcadia in Botetourt County. Part of the Jefferson National Forest, this is a popular spot for trout fishing.

Above: Along a section of the Massanutten Mountain West Trail between Edinburg and Woodstock gaps, a hiker is rewarded with spectacular views of the Valley and the Shenandoah River bends (called Seven Bends) below.

Facing page: In Alleghany and Bath counties, Lake Moomaw (along with the Gathright Dam) was created to maintain flood control and water quality along the James and Jackson rivers. The lake and recreation area, part of George Washington National Forest, provide abundant opportunities for boating, fishing, camping, and hiking.

Above: A lone visitor marvels at Giant's Hall in Luray Caverns, the eastern United States' largest caverns.

Left: Dating from 1761, Jefferson Pools at Warm Springs in Bath County is the oldest of Virginia's famed hot springs resorts. Among those enjoying the medicinal waters was Thomas Jefferson.

Above: Canning remains essential to many Valley families. Here, the results of their efforts are displayed at the Rockingham County Agricultural Fair.

Right: Warren County Courthouse, Front Royal. Interstate 66, a main artery from Washington and northern Virginia, passes through the county, bringing visitors to the Valley and to Shenandoah National Park, the north entrance of which is at Front Royal.

Above: Referred to as "the Breadbasket of the Confederacy" during the Civil War, the Valley supplied much of the Southern army's food supplies. After Union troops undertook a campaign to destroy the Valley's agricultural infrastructure, the Baylor Mill near Swoope in Augusta County was one of the few mills left standing.

Left: Dairy farms like this one near Bridgewater are plentiful in Rockingham County, which ranks first in the state in agriculture.

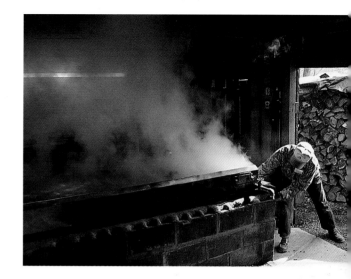

Above: At Eagle's Sugar Camp in Highland County, a farmer tends to boiling sugar. During the wildly popular annual Maple Sugar Festival, visitors can watch the syrup-making process on tours of the county's sugar camps.

Left: The Natural Bridge of Virginia in Rockbridge County, once owned by Thomas Jefferson, is a mammoth limestone arch 90 feet wide and 215 feet high. In 1750, a young George Washington carved his initials in the bridge while surveying the area.

Facing page: Union and Confederate soldiers face off on the battlefield at a reenactment of the Battle of New Market.

Above: A frosty morning dawns at Silver Lake near Dayton in Rockingham County.

Right: A barn near Cross Keys in Rockingham County is framed by the pink blossoms of a dogwood, Virginia's state tree.

Above: While they occupied the village of McDowell in Highland County during the Civil War, Union soldiers carved this graffiti into the brick walls of the Presbyterian church.

Left: Downtown Staunton's skyline, with its impressive period architecture, is one of the most striking in the Valley. The city's unique shops, restaurants, and bed-and-breakfasts, as well as its highly praised Blackfriars Playhouse, make Staunton a unique getaway destination.

Above: A dancer in Seminole costume performs at a powwow held near Quicksburg in Rockingham County.

Right: A farmer's dog keeps him company while he works in a field near Montezuma in Rockingham County.

Above: Peaches ripen in the late-summer sun at an orchard in Berkeley County, West Virginia.

Left: Along Route 11, the old Valley Pike, near Meems Bottom in Shenandoah County, the morning sun peeks around the branches of an old tree. In the distance, a farm lies at the foot of Massanutten Mountain.

Facing page: A lily pond captures the reflection of historic Edgewater Manor in Bunkerhill, West Virginia. Built in 1839 for John Boyd, Sr., the property saw a lot of action during the Civil War. John Boyd, Jr., was captured here by Union soldiers and charged as a spy, and Stonewall Jackson used the estate's lawn as a camp.

Above: During the McDowell Battlefield Heritage Days, the whole village gets involved when hundreds of men, women, and children in period costumes act out the May 1862 Union occupation.

Right: A grazing sheep flock adds to this bucolic scene as dusk settles over Highland County, near Monterey.

Pat and Chuck Blackley

Pat and Chuck Blackley are a photographic and writing team who work throughout North America but make their home in the Shenandoah Valley of Virginia. The Valley and surrounding mountains are favorite photographic subjects.

The Blackleys' work appears in numerous magazines, including *Backpacker, Blue Ridge Country, Country, Endless Vacation, Family Fun, Frommer's Budget Travel, Outdoor Photographer,* and *Travel America,* and in books by Countryman Press, Farcountry Press, Frommer's, Insight Guides, National Geographic, Reader's Digest, and Ulysses Press. Additionally, their photographs appear regularly in calendars, commercial projects, and other publications by organizations such as Avalanche Press, Impact Photographics, KC Publications, National Park Service, Pace Communications, Sierra Club, and the Wilderness Society.

Their previous works for Farcountry Press are *Shenandoah National Park Impressions* and *Blue Ridge Parkway Impressions.*